Who's Your Hubby?

Tips for Living Happily with 10 Hubby Types

Beth Rabinowitz

and

Monica Schaeffer, Ph.D.

First published by Dog Ear Publishing
4010 W. 86th Street, Ste H
Indianapolis, IN 46268
www.dogearpublishing.net

ISBN: 978-1-4575-1635-1

This book is printed on acid-free paper.

Printed in the United States of America

www.whosyourhubby.com

Table of Contents

Dedication

To our hubbies, Ken and Mitch, who were the inspiration for our different hubby types — you can guess which ones! You've given us inspiration, frustration, and many, many laughs along the way. We wouldn't want to go through life's journey with anyone else.

To our mothers, Ronia and Lilo, and our fathers, David and Hans — our role models for sustained love and for engaging in behaviors mostly to follow, but a few to avoid!

To our children, Jason and Elana, and Erica, Jodie, and Lacey — we hope the words on these pages will help you enter marriage with a repertoire of coping strategies you can call upon to make the words "living happily ever after" a blissful reality.

What Our Mothers Told Us (and Didn't Tell Us)

Our mothers told us: "You can't live with them, and you can't live without them!" What our mothers didn't tell us is how to live with them. For that, we need each other. Just as we've shared cooking recipes in the past, we can now share recipes for marital success.

After more than 60 years of marriage between the two of us and after interviewing women with over 1,000 collective years of marriage, we have concluded that our mothers did not have all the tips that are provided in this book!

You will find these "tips," or strategies, organized around ten hubby types. Our survey indicated these to be the most challenging hubby types, our "Hubby Top Ten." These strategies are from the pros — women who average more than 25 years of marriage each; and who, for more than 90%, indicated this was their first and only marriage.

We've dedicated a chapter to each of these types of hubbies:

* Chubby Hubby
* Non-Communicative Hubby
* Sportsaholic Hubby
* Unfashionable Hubby (aka Bad Dresser)
* Domestically Challenged Hubby
* Frugal Hubby
* Unromantic Hubby
* Workaholic Hubby
* Time-Insensitive Hubby
* Messy Hubby

While no one can know for certain if a current or potential hubby will morph into one of our Hubby Top Tens, we have included warning signs in each chapter that may help you predict your hubby's future path. They're not foolproof, however; these are just some general guidelines that may predict the challenges you could potentially face.

In many of these cases, wives told us that *they* were the ones who had changed their outlook or perspective and chose to do something for themselves, so we have concluded each hubby chapter with these tips.

While you may want to read only about a specific hubby type, please be sure to read the last chapter, "Cupid's Cheat Sheet." This chapter summarizes what we heard from women when asked about what practical advice they would give to newlyweds. This advice is just as good for "olderweds" who might need to recharge their marriage batteries!

We thought it only fair that we would give our hubbies a voice in this book, so check out the chapter entitled "Why Nagging Doesn't Work." Of course, we couldn't give them the last word, so their contributions are followed by the chapter "Why Ignoring It Doesn't Work."

In summary, we wrote this book to help newlyweds, "olderweds," and soon-to-be-weds joyfully live together. So newlyweds and soon-to-be-weds, to put you ahead of the learning curve, and "olderweds," before you think about leaving your hubbies, see how these women learned to live happily *with* their hubbies, not *without* them.

Why Nagging Doesn't Work (The Hubbies' Chapter)

A psychiatrist asks a lot of expensive questions your wife asks for nothing.

—Joey Adams

Our wives finally seem to have come to grips with the fact that after 30+ years of marriage, we haven't really done much to change the worst part of our personalities — at least, not to any great degree. We're not suggesting that we can't change for the better. We're not suggesting that at all. We think we are better hubbies today than we were after the honeymoon period wore off.

We do know that nagging us doesn't work, however. We don't really know why, but here is our take on it: It seems to us that in order to get someone to do something that he doesn't necessarily want to do, that is not a priority, that person must in some way be motivated to leap into action.

Nagging is like squeaky chalk on a blackboard. Nagging is probably one of the oldest forms of torture. A man would do anything to get it to stop; anything, that is, but the one thing that his wife is nagging him to do.

Maybe this reaction is a sort of masochism. We hope not, because we don't want to be masochists — that would mean that we want our wives to continue to nag us about the little things that she wants done on her time, those things that are a priority to her, but not to us. We haven't studied torture, but if nagging is similar, we think one of the basic reasons it doesn't usually work for us is because we have been able to build up our "nagging immune system."

We know this analogy is leaning toward the ridiculous, but when someone is beaten repeatedly over time, he develops calluses. Being beaten or whipped is never anything but a horrible, inhumane experience, but we would guess that those calluses may create some kind of minimal barrier that would make further torture less effective.

Husbands have been able to build calluses in their brains that cause words at a certain pitch and decibel level not to reach the receptors. This makes it nearly impossible to go into action. Notice, we did not say *absolutely* impossible: Nagging does work on rare occasions. We have not found the key to what triggers a proper action and desired reaction, however. It is a very complicated subject, and a great deal more research is needed in this area.

Because this protective shield is built up over many years, one cannot expect different results from the same repeated action. It is like Albert Einstein said about the definition of insanity: it is repeating the same thing over and over, but expecting different results.

We think there is an inverse correlation between the amount of nagging that is done and the likelihood of it being successful. Nagging becomes less and less effective as a tactic over time. Look, we are to a point where we both know it doesn't work, so it has become somewhat of a ritual: She nags. He acknowledges. He gets distracted. She simmers. Then the cycle starts again.

This cycle is part of the natural circle of life. If men went into action right away, we would be breaking a long-standing tradition, one that has withstood the test of time, between husband and wife. Who are we to buck the system?

Seriously, though, sometimes our priorities are just not aligned. It is not that we don't have the same priorities. Frankly, most of the things that are on our wives' lists are also on our lists: painting, putting the lid down, getting the oil changed, and shopping for something (anything). It is just that we have some additional things on our lists: watching the game, watching the post-game show, and watching the highlights of the game. So our lists are longer than our wives' lists, and the pecking order of things are a little different, of course, first things first. Other than that, we are completely aligned.

What to do? We wish we could help. We can't, but we'll try our best. Here it is. Here is everything we have...don't nag. Do anything else, but nag.

- *Ask once, nicely. (You have tried that and it didn't work, well keep trying it. It may not work, but at least it will be more pleasant.)*
- *Decide whether you should even ask at all. Is it really that important?*
- *Do something nice for him first. (There is a chance our wives may have tried that one.)*
- *Concentrate on your hubby's strengths, not weaknesses. Nagging is really focusing on areas where your husband is an underachiever. It's much easier to strengthen our strengths than to strengthen our weaknesses.*
- *Finally, would you consider doing it yourself? (We just thought we would ask.)*

When we think of a world without nagging, we hear that Louis Armstrong song rolling around in our heads: "What a wonderful world"... it would be. Oh, yeah!

Why Ignoring It Doesn't Work

"What counts in making a happy marriage is not so much how compatible you are, but how you deal with incompatibility."

—George Levinger

You have heard from the hubbies on why nagging, whining, and threatening do not work. Now you need to know that ignoring the problem/issues won't work, either.

At first, the issues might seem small and not worth mentioning. For instance, your hubby may leave his socks or his clothes wherever he drops them and doesn't put them in the hamper or hang them in the closet. So you pick up after him because you don't want a messy house. Or he doesn't call you to let you know that he will be late until five minutes before he said he would be home, You are so busy with the kids that you let this go as well. The list goes on and on.

You think that any one of these is not a serious issue. You are correct — any one of these is no big deal. All of these "daily hassles" do mount up, though, and before you realize it, you have lost your ability to contain your frustration, and you end up going ballistic. Your hubby looks at you as if you are from another planet and wonders how you can be so unreasonable. He does not get that your actions are a culmination of many little hassles bundled together.

We are here to try to prevent you from blowing your stack. One important step is to recognize that ignoring the things that bother you about your hubby is harmful to your relationship. Rather than dismissing them, they should be dealt with in a timely matter. Recognize that it is a two-way street, however, and allow your hubby to voice things that you do that might be bothering him, as well.

Most of all, do not despair. Read each chapter for strategies that have been used successfully by other wives.

These strategies will help you remember why you said, "I do."

We promise!

Chubby Hubby

"People shop for a bathing suit with more care than they do for a husband or wife. The rules are the same. Look for something you'll feel comfortable wearing. Allow room to grow."

—Erma Brombeck

Chubby When We First Met

First, it was finding the crumpled candy wrappers wedged between the car seats or under the driver's seat of his car. Then, it was the bags of cookies in the pantry with only a few cookies left. I had a closet eater on my hands who denied it whenever confronted!

This went on for years. I knew my husband had a stressful job, so I didn't want to say too much, but after gaining 50 pounds, I regretted not nipping it in the bud.

Chubby Later On

When I first started dating my husband in college, I was amazed by the amount he could eat: two double cheeseburgers, french fries, a milkshake, and that was just a late-night snack! I wasn't concerned then, because he had such a good physique.

Fast track 20 years later—he has the same eating habits, but certainly not the same physique! Evidently, his metabolism has not kept up with his appetite!

Over the years, we've tried a number of strategies to uncover the healthy hubby that lies beneath those particularly large love handles.

Chubby Warning Signs

Will I Be Married to a Chubby Hubby?

- What does he like to eat, high-carb killers like potatoes and pasta or healthy foods like fruits and vegetables?
- What about his portion control? Does he overload his plate and always have more than one helping?
- Is snacking a problem? Are the peanuts, popcorn, and candy always out?
- Is he a couch potato? Does he participate in sports/activities or just watch them on TV?
- Does he belong to a health club/gym? Does he work out regularly?
- Is his family, especially his father, overweight?

Chubby Strategies

Enlisting the Troops

If and when your words or tears are no longer effective and you have children, enlist your kids to alter your hubby's eating habits. Young kids can (with your supervision) put healthy snacks in a paper bag along with a handwritten note or illustration telling your hubby to have a healthy, happy day at work. These can be slipped into his briefcase or car before he leaves for work. Older kids can share with your hubby what his weight gain or bad eating habits mean to them.

One daughter routinely tells her dad how unfair he is being to the family by causing family members to worry and be stressed. She has also mentioned that his weight is something he has control over, unlike an illness, but he chooses not to exert that control. One son regularly e-mails his dad articles and links to diet web sites.

When kids take the time to sit down for a chat, hubbies usually respond with a sincere, renewed effort. Since these efforts are short-lived, however, you might try coupling this strategy with some of the other ones listed.

Shopping Cart & Meal Plan

Bad eating habits are hard to break. One way to begin breaking these habits is to go shopping together in order to help your hubby start reading labels for calories, fat, and sugar content. Have him compare the labels from his favorite snacks with those from healthy ones. Try cooking a meal together so he can see how easy it is to eat healthy. In one case we know of, the hubby got so into this that he was cooking one meal a week!

Role Models

Who knew that reality TV could serve a purpose? More than one hubby has gotten into watching *The Biggest Loser* with his spouse and has lost weight because of it. The message these men seem to be taking away from this show is, "If they can do it, I can do it." It must be something about the competition, since most men love to win.

Role models, whether they are reality TV competitors or others that you can think of, help your hubby stay focused on his own weight-loss goal. Make sure that when you're watching TV together, you have healthy snacks he can reach for.

Professional Touch

Doctors can have a strong influence over hubbies if you can get them to go see one. The key is finding the right doctor. Researching the best doctor will need to be your job. Whatever you do, don't have your hubby go to a friend, especially a male doctor friend—he will buy into your hubby's story about how hard he is trying, but how he just can't seem to do it.

While we hate to sound sexist, in our experience, female doctors try harder to convince men to lose weight and follow-up to see that hubbies are doing what they promised to do. Go with your hubby for the first few appointments, even if he puts up a fuss. Too many wives have told us that their hubbies' retention of what needs to be done is filled with holes. You can be there to support him in following doctor's orders.

Buddy System

As we said, men love to compete, so the buddy system often works well in losing weight. In one long-distance situation, two wives whose hubbies were not having success losing weight by themselves got together. The wives each kept track of their respective spouses' weekly weight, but did not share this information with the buddy. The hubbies both researched different ways to lose weight and actually had fun sharing these methods with their buddy.

At the end of every quarter of the year, the wives scheduled a weekend together to reveal the results. The hubby who lost the most weight got treated to a movie, dinner, or something else that was seen as a prize. Both hubbies ended up losing a significant amount of weight while keeping up their long-distance friendship.

Professional Program

When he has not had success with any of the strategies that he has tried on his own or with the help of friends and family members be sure he does not give up. There are many professional programs that can serve as jumpstarts for embarking on a healthy lifestyle. The key to their success is that they need to be easily accessible, provide monitoring of your hubby's progress, and include a component that makes your hubby know he is accountable to someone who has his best interests in mind.

Some hubbies might be willing to see a nutritionist, who can evaluate his eating habits and monitor his progress. Other hubbies might benefit from going away to structured programs for 2–3 weeks. When this amount of time is just too much time away from work or family, local programs exist to keep your hubby in line. These programs often include not only physical exams, but talks and coaching with nutritionists, behavioral specialists, and trainers.

In addition to being used as jumpstarts, these programs can be revisited quarterly or annually to get your hubby through some tough times.

"Exercise Diet"

Exercise is a key component to losing weight. Playing a sport is an effective way to incorporate exercise into your hubby's routine. In one case, even though a membership to the tennis club was expensive, both wife and hubby could see the benefit in weight loss. They jokingly referred to this summer period as his "annual tennis diet."

Whether he chooses a competitive sport or individual exercise, be there to help your hubby find a way to exercise consistently at a convenient place and time.

Awards Ceremony

Anyone who has tried to lose weight knows how critical positive reinforcement is to success. Find out ahead of time what your hubby would see as a reward for reaching different milestones. A word of caution, though: make sure you can implement these rewards when he reaches his milestones. Also, remember to make a big deal of his progress by communicating how good it makes you feel.

Class Reunion

Any special occasion can be used as a motivator for your hubby to lose weight. You can bring out old pictures of him at past family celebrations as ammunition for him to change. While weddings, anniversaries, Bar Mitzvahs, or confirmations can be the impetus for change, there's nothing like a class reunion to inspire a crash diet.

The secret here is to begin planning the diet well in advance and to have strategies in place for maintaining the weight loss afterward.

Do Something for Yourself!

While the goal is to improve your hubby's health with the strategies listed above, there may be times when you feel frustrated by your attempts to modify his habits. When this happens, it is time to do something that you have direct control over!

For example, make sure that you are eating healthy foods and working exercise into your daily routine. Also, eliminate those tasty, but unhealthy, snacks from your cupboard. Many wives have seen this to be a successful strategy—they feel much better about themselves and many hubbies have "followed the leader," losing weight themselves!

Chubby Checklist

- ☑ *Enlisting the Troops*
- ☑ *Shopping Cart & Meal Plan*
- ☑ *Role Models*
- ☑ *Professional Touch*
- ☑ *Buddy System*
- ☑ *Professional Program*
- ☑ *"Exercise Diet"*
- ☑ *Awards Ceremony*
- ☑ *Class Reunion*

Non-Communicative Hubby

"My wife says I never listen to her. At least I think that's what she said."

—Francis Rodman

When we were first married, it seemed so nice. We could be driving in the car, totally silent. I remember thinking that with most people this silence would feel totally awkward, each person trying to figure out what to say. So, for many years there was this feeling of bliss.

But slowly it started to bother me. I was the one initiating all the conversations and getting back yes or no answers, even with open-ended questions! I sometimes would time how long we could go without saying a word—way too long!

Ladies, don't despair. In this chapter, you will find ways to open up and clear the static from your hubby communication lines.

Non-Communicative Warning Signs

Will I Be Married to a Non-Communicative Hubby?

- Who initiates the conversation? Is it always you?
- Are there long moments of silence in your conversations?
- Do you struggle to find topics to talk about?
- Do you often eat meals or travel in silence?
- Are you surprised to learn things you didn't know about your hubby from his friends? His family?

Non-Communicative Strategies

Start Your Own Book Club

Instead of getting frustrated about your hubby's failure to communicate, suggest that just the two of you start a "book club." Take turns selecting the book-of-the-month. This is a novel way to engage your hubby on a whole range of topics.

As a way to "break the ice" you can innocently ask questions about how your hubby might handle a particular situation or what he admires most about one of the characters.

One couple went from reading *Freakenomics to The Girl with the Dragon Tattoo.* Even after more than 30 years of marriage, each one found out new things about the other. Talking about the book served as a springboard for increasingly lively conversation not only at the dinner table and in the car, but also in bed!

Make A List

One wife reports that her hubby hardly talks at all while they are driving in the car. He claims he is concentrating on the road but she knows his mind is on his business. So she came up with a list of possible topics, and then they agreed on the categories they would talk about. She keeps the list in the glove compartment so it is handy when needed.

Play A Game

Since men are so competitive, it might be fun to play a game with your hubby.

Ask your hubby to name something that makes you feel good, safe, happy, or sad. You could ask him about your favorite author, food, movie, or TV show. You must also answer the questions about what makes him feel good, safe, etc. If the questioner agrees with any of the answers given, the respondent gets a point. Keep a running tab of your points to figure out who gets to 21 first, and that person gets to ask the spouse for a favor.

Anniversary Countdown

Anniversaries are a good time to communicate the qualities you both cherish about each other. If you start this early, it will automatically become a part of celebrating your special day.

Forget the store-bought card. Each of you can write your own by completing the following thoughts:

- **What I love about you most is....**
- **The kindest thing you've done for me this year is...**
- **A special time we shared this year was...**
- **I married you because...**

Date these and keep them in a book; that way, you can see over time how the responses change. Not only will you have created a keepsake, but you will realize that what you have is worth holding onto for years to come.

Reconnect

Part of the reason for your hubby being non-communicative may be the pressures he is under. Many men have a difficult time sharing their worries with their wives — or anyone, for that matter. You need to break the deadlock and find ways to relieve your hubby's pressure. Make sure he knows that you can be his confidante.

Don't expect him to open up the minute he comes home from work, however. He needs to decompress and have some time to himself, even if you are ready to tear your hair out because of your busy day. Patience on your part will end up being more profitable than lashing out at your hubby.

Both of you should agree on a set time that is devoted to talking to each other, and then guard against this time together becoming a chore. Start with an "ice-breaker" — such as a funny joke or an inspirational message. You can find plenty of these either by googling for ideas or finding an inspirational book filled with short messages or sayings.

While reconnecting every day is the best strategy, you should make sure that you have at least one evening each week you can count on to talk and really listen to each other.

Do Something for Yourself!

Don't put wind in your angry sails. Along with trying the strategies we've listed above, use some of the quiet time between the two of you to make phone calls to friends or complete your list of things you need to do.

By getting involved in another activity of your own, whether it is a hobby or some philanthropic endeavor, your own self-worth will be boosted and the quiet time between the two of you might not feel so threatening to your relationship.

Non-Communicative Checklist

- ☑ *Start Your Own Book Club*
- ☑ *Make a List*
- ☑ *Play a Game*
- ☑ *Anniversary Countdown*
- ☑ *Reconnect*

Sportsaholic Hubby

"If you're a sports fan you realize that when you meet somebody, like a girlfriend, they kind of have to root for your team. They don't have a choice."

—Jimmy Fallon

I knew this might be a problem area when on one of our first dates, we went to the movies, and I discovered he had an earphone in his ear (on the side away from me) so he wouldn't miss the last quarter of a NY Knicks game! My tale of woe gets worse from thereon in: a radio, TV, or tablet accompanies us almost everywhere we go. Through miles of travel (and tons of static), we're almost always listening to something sports related.

That's the spectator part, but I have to deal with the participant part, as well. Over the years, his home away from home has become our local tennis club. With more leisure time as his workload has decreased, he "holds court" at the club, playing tennis, "schmoozing," playing tennis, and schmoozing some more. Some days he can be there from dawn to dusk.

Fearful that your Sportsaholic Hubby will never be around to "play" with you again? Put the ball back in your court by following the strategies we recommend.

Sportsaholic Warning Signs

Will I Be Married to a Sportsaholic Hubby?

- Are sports an unusually large part of his life? Are they the most important part of his life?
- Does he obsess about the big game?
- Does he have to watch/read everything about his teams?
- Is he unwilling to leave until the game is over?
- Do you have to juggle appointments to meet his game schedule?

Sportsaholic Strategies

If You Can't Beat 'Em, Join 'Em!

Even if you were never interested in sports before, learning about a particular sport (or sports) your hubby loves can reap dividends for both of you.

One wife told us that even though she was a cheerleader in high school, she never really understood football until she started watching games with a girlfriend while both their husbands were away on business trips. Both soon became football fanatics, studying their team rosters, reading newspaper articles, watching ESPN, and even attending a football camp for women at their team's summer training camp! Now they have a great hobby, and the fact that they share it with their hubbies makes it even better.

So whatever sport your hubby is into, why not give it a chance? The more you learn about it, the more you may really like it. It can become a good way for you and your hubby to share quality time together.

Become a Soccer Mom

If your hubby is a sportsaholic, chances are that your children will be into sports as well. Even mothers with no athletic ability whatsoever can become fanatics when watching their own kids slamming baseballs or kicking soccer balls. Learn the rules of the sports your children play so you can become a knowledgeable fan and cheer at the appropriate times on the sidelines.

Attending your children's sporting events can become a fun and rewarding pastime. You'll make new friends with the other parents and, depending on the sport, get some fresh air and exercise. You may even travel to some new and exotic places!

Record It!

Thank goodness for digital recording technology! With this great invention, your hubby can record all his favorite sporting events and you can both attend social activities that are important to you.

Timing is important, though. You'll get "pushback" if there's any chance he'll hear the score prior to being able to watch the big game. If you want your hubby to embrace this device that can help save your social life, you need to be diligent in guarding against score announcements.

First, make sure you monitor incoming information. When answering phone calls from other sportsaholics, make sure they know that your hubby hasn't watched the game yet, and that they shouldn't tell him anything about it. After you've programmed the recording, make sure you change the channel so when you put on live TV upon your return home, you don't accidentally tune it to the end of the big game!

Sports Planner

Most Sportsaholic hubbies will vehemently deny that their sports habits are out of control. Use your planning skills to prove your case and to help him put limits on his sports-viewing passion.

At the beginning of each week, "map out" the programs he plans to watch day by day and add up the percentage of free time (non-working, non-chore related, non-previously scheduled) this viewing would take up. For example, if between transporting the kids to activities and household chores you have approximately 20 "free" hours per week (2 hours each weeknight and 12 hours each weekend) and he's spending close to 75% of that time watching sports (2 football games on Sunday, and 2 to 3 football/basketball/hockey games during the week), hopefully he will see that there is a problem!

Together, you need to agree to reduce these hours to a "manageable" percentage. For the games he agrees to "cut," he can use the "Record It" strategy…Just make sure he doesn't watch them during the time you've dedicated to be together!

No Couch Potatoes Allowed!

While we know men are not multitaskers, especially when watching their favorite sports channels, let your hubby know that he can enjoy his games without interruption from you if he agrees to accomplish at least one or two things while watching.

Start him off with easy tasks such as folding the laundry or putting a load in the washer or dryer during halftime and commercials. As an alternative, to help hubbies keep in shape, some wives have reported success in getting their hubbies to use the treadmill or lift weights while watching sports.

Remember to give him positive strokes on his initiatives to increase the possibility that he will continue to be an active viewer rather than a couch potato.

Do Something for Yourself!

He's spending time with the guys, so now it's your turn to spend time with the girls! Plan something with your friends during the big game.

How about a day at the spa or a dinner at your favorite restaurant? Perhaps you could join a book club? There are so many options to choose from, but choose wisely. Make sure it's something you really enjoy. You'll be happy his "sportsaholicism" gave you this opportunity!

Sportsaholic Checklist

- ☑ *If you Can't Beat 'Em, Join 'Em*
- ☑ *Become a Soccer Mom*
- ☑ *Record It!*
- ☑ *Sports Planner*
- ☑ *No Couch Potatoes Allowed!*

Unfashionable Hubby (aka Bad Dresser)

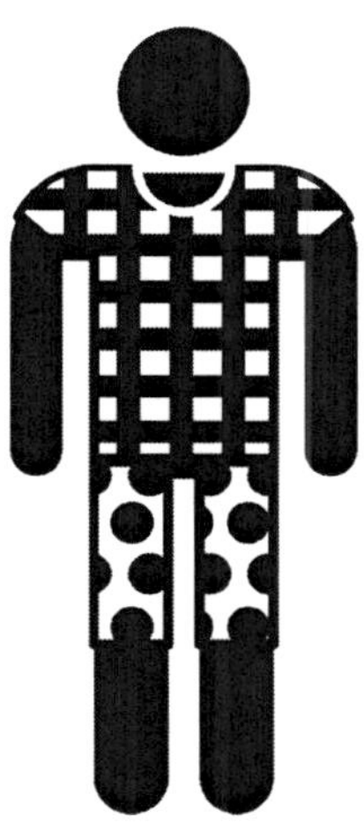

"A good marriage would be between a blind wife and a deaf husband."

—Honore de Balzac

I know I shouldn't be concerned about what other people think about how my husband and I look, but I'm a woman; I can't help it! So, when my husband decks himself out in a shirt and pants that clash or an outfit that looks like he stepped right out of the 70s (or 60s, or even 50s), I do get upset.

He wasn't like this when we first met; he always looked nice and dressed fashionably. Maybe the dress choices on a college campus weren't too difficult, or maybe back then he still wanted to impress me.

Over the years his clothing choices have gotten worse and worse and he has gotten more and more stubborn about taking fashion advice. I think he takes it as an affront to his masculinity that I should make suggestions on what he should wear, as well as to his maturity. (You're treating me like a child — no, a child would dress better than you do.)

Worried you'll never be able to go out in public with your unfashionable hubby again? Never fear! We have strategies that could put him in GQ, or at least make him presentable.

Unfashionable Warning Signs

Will I Be Married to an Unfashionable Hubby?

- How does he dress now?
- Do his shirts and pants match?
- Are his outfits coordinated? Does he wear the right shoes, belts, etc?
- Does he wear the same clothes over and over? Are they frayed and worn-out?
- How's his sense of style? Is he stuck in the 70s, 80s, or 90s?
- How does his father dress?
- Do his parents fight over what your father-in-law is wearing?

Unfashionable Strategies

Buy His Clothes

Most unfashionable hubbies don't like clothes and don't like shopping for clothes, so they'll be very happy if you do the shopping for them. Make sure you give him several choices when you bring clothes home for him to try on. This way, the final decision is still his. Otherwise he may rebel, even though he might secretly like everything you picked out. With you in control of the shopping, you can ensure his choices are fashionable and up-to-date. Most unfashionable hubbies will be happy if they never have to go shopping again!

Shop Together

You might have to drag him kicking and screaming to the store, but this is much less dangerous than letting your unfashionable hubby shop for himself. You know how that will turn out! Make the shopping together as enjoyable as possible. Maybe you could even combine it with something he really likes to do like dinner or a movie?

Shop with the Kids

If you're lucky enough to have a teenager or older son or daughter who inherited your fashion sense and not their father's, send them shopping with their dad. Your unfashionable hubby may be more willing to take fashion advice from his offspring than his spouse and this could be a fun father-son or father-daughter activity. Remember, though, to coach your son or daughter beforehand if there are certain items you want them to stay away from!

Clean (Weed out) His Closet

Maybe there are fashionable gems in his closet, but your hubby just can't seem to find them because they're hidden behind all the out-of-date, worn-out, and just plain ugly items. Or maybe your hubby has some really nice clothes, but never wears them because he insists on wearing his old favorites that you just can't stand? If that's the case, "store" the offending items in some out of the way area where your hubby is not likely to look. Now when he opens his closet, he'll only see (and wear) the items you approve or mostly approve of.

Buy Him a "Dress for Success" Book

Is your hubby employed in a job where his appearance could affect his chances for advancement? Does he not place enough importance on this aspect of his career? There are numerous books available that will help make him a "believer" and possibly a fashion-maven, as well. If you can get your hubby to read it, this could be the breakthrough you need. Your hubby doesn't read much? Try placing a GQ-type magazine in strategic locations, such as his night table, where he might take the time to thumb through them or pick up some tips through osmosis!

Do Something for Yourself!

There's no reason why you can't be a fashion plate just because your hubby isn't!

If you enjoy looking well put together, continue to spend the time and money to do so. You'll feel good about yourself, and everyone will know your hubby's fashion problems are truly his own, and have nothing to do with you!

Unfashionable Checklist

☑ *Buy His Clothes*

☑ *Shop Together*

☑ *Shop with the Kids*

☑ *Clean (Weed Out) His Closet*

☑ *Buy Him a "Dress for Success" Book*

Domestically Challenged Hubby

"A husband is someone who takes out the trash and gives the impression he just cleaned the whole house."

—Author unknown

I knew I might be in trouble when I attended my first dinner party at my in-laws' house. Dinner was served buffet style that night, and even though all the other guests went into the family room to fill their plates, my father-in-law stayed seated at the head of the dining room table and my mother-in-law brought a filled dinner plate to him!

Even though this was many years ago, and traditional marriages were much more in vogue back then, I was more than a little concerned, and rightfully so, about my husband's "King of the Castle" role model.

Learn how to get your hubby off his throne and doing his fair share of castle repair and maintenance.

Domestically Challenged Warning Signs

Will I Be Married to a Domestically Challenged Hubby?

- How helpful is he now?
- Does he help prepare dinner or set or clear the table?
- Does he do the dishes?
- Does he make household repairs?
- Did he do chores growing up?
- Does he make his bed?
- Did his father help out around the house?
- Does he know how to cook?

Domestically Challenged Strategies

Do It Together

As newlyweds, set ground rules for home chores. Part of the stress in doing anything around the house is that wives find themselves doing it alone while their hubbies watch TV, read the paper, or claim they need to "work."

Decide on a time and day each week when you will both tackle the major cleaning chores. Misery loves miserable company; you will find that being in the same boat and tackling the cleaning together will not only lead to less resentment on your part, but also result in a feeling of satisfaction and pride in your mutual accomplishments. Put on some music and take some breaks to make these chores more tolerable.

You built this home together, and maintaining it together will lead to more harmony.

Negotiate Tasks—List and Rank

Since getting your hubby to participate in house chores is your goal, sometimes you might need to negotiate tasks.

Schedule a time when you can talk about the tasks that need to get done. List them on a board or spreadsheet so that both of you can see the total number of tasks. Rank them in importance and frequency and then make "assignments" for each.

If certain jobs like cleaning the bathroom toilets get no takers, you will need to negotiate and compromise on how often each person takes on these tasks. By taking this step, you might convince your hubby sooner rather than later of the benefits of hiring someone to help with the list!

Divide & Conquer

After negotiating tasks, you'll need to find ways to see that they get done.

While many wives believe that household chores go more quickly if they do them themselves rather than arguing with their spouses about the right way to do something, in the long run, this strategy can lead to more frustration and resentment.

Hubbies will try to claim they are ill-equipped to do a good job such as making the bed to your specifications, but don't let them win. Be patient and show them the steps, then let them do it while you watch. Don't be a perfectionist. Recognize that in making the bed, most men view pillows as functional, not decorative. It's easier to fix things later rather than doing everything yourself first. Also, ask your hubby to show you something that he usually takes care of around the house so that he knows this is a two-way street!

As for the day-to-day chores, such as cooking, cleaning up after eating, hanging up coats, and folding laundry, make sure you both know who is responsible for getting these done. Alternate days or chores so neither one of you gets stuck with the worst jobs.

Hire Someone

You have seen this strategy recommended for other types of hubbies, but for a domestically challenged hubby, this is a priority! Many wives have told us they have given up new pairs of shoes or lunches with their friends to get the relief that comes from walking into a clean, organized home.

Make sure to have this as a line-item in your budget as soon as you can afford it. One wife extends the enjoyment of one day off from house cleaning or "straightening up" by not cooking dinner on the day she has her house cleaned.

Little Black Book

To prevent yourself from blowing your top, ask your friends and family for names and numbers of plumbers, painters, electricians, and handymen and keep them in a handy place. Do this before a crisis occurs. Having dependable people at the ready can save you time, money, and exasperation with your spouse.

If he's the type that wants to do everything himself, set the ground rules early. Strike an agreement with him that states that after asking him three times to do something, you have the right to call someone to get the job done.

Do Something for Yourself!

Since keeping communication channels open and finding the time to do things as a couple is key to a happy marriage, consider signing up for a class that is focused on a household chore together or with another couple.

For example, enrolling both of you in a cooking or landscaping class may awaken a talent your hubby did not know he possessed. At a minimum, he will be more willing to take ownership of a task and no longer view it just as a chore, but as a new skill he can dazzle you and others with. Most importantly, you will be able to cross something off your list!

Domestically Challenged Checklist

- ☑ ***Do It Together***
- ☑ ***Negotiate Tasks—List and Rank***
- ☑ ***Divide & Conquer***
- ☑ ***Hire Someone***
- ☑ ***Little Black Book***

Frugal Hubby

Marriage halves our griefs, doubles our joys, and quadruples our expenses.

—English proverb

My husband has always made a good living and we can afford many of the finer things in life; he just doesn't like to pay full price for them. And since he doesn't know the difference between good quality and "schlock," especially when it comes to clothing, furniture, or jewelry, we often get into heated discussions (fights) over whether or not we really need to buy the more expensive (higher quality) items.

Of course, this doesn't apply to his "toys." He always has to have the latest and best in technology and sports equipment. It just applies to the things I want to buy — quality as well as quantity. "Why do I need (or want) more than one pair of earrings, bracelet, or necklace — you can't wear more than one at a time." The sad part is, I think he was serious!

Don't worry. You don't have to buy all your household goods at the flea market if you follow our advice on how to loosen your frugal hubby's purse strings.

Frugal Warning Signs

Will I Be Married to a Frugal Hubby?

- **What types of dates did you go on? Did he take you to nice restaurants or cheap joints?**
- **Does he give you sensible gifts? It will only get worse over time!**
- **Did you receive a plant on Valentine's Day rather than flowers because plants last longer?**
- **Does he always look for bargains?**
- **Does he spend an inordinate amount of time comparison shopping for even the most insignificant items?**
- **Does he ever buy luxury items, or does he only buy things that are reasonable?**
- **What about his attitude toward quality? Is it only the price of something that matters to him?**

Frugal Strategies

Look for Bargains

Even if bargain hunting is not in your nature, demonstrating that you can be frugal will go a long way to loosening your frugal hubby's purse strings in other areas. When you find a bargain, make sure you brag about your shopping prowess — he'll be so proud of you!

Don't have time for bargain hunting? Some bargains are really easy to come by. Don't you always need something at Bed Bath & Beyond? They constantly mail out special coupons, and you can find the coupons in the newspaper, as well.

Many coupon sites exist online. Before shopping, check the websites of retail stores for coupons you can print out or show retailers on your smart phone. Apps like RedLaser allow you to see if you are getting the best deal by scanning the barcode of your item.

How about making sure you return your movie rentals on time? It might be only a few dollars saved, but your frugal hubby will sit up and take notice.

Financial Planning 101

There are actually two components to this strategy: establishing ground rules and scheduling regular budget reviews.

First of all, even though it may be difficult, you need to get on the same financial page. Come up with a household budget together so you know, and agree upon, what you are spending. If there are some discretionary funds left over, both of you need to agree on how they will be used. The fixed-price items, for example, mortgage/rent, utilities, and car payments, are easy. It's the non-fixed price items, such as clothing, furniture, and gifts that usually cause the most problems. If you agree on a budget amount, however, and you stay within that budget, then your frugal hubby should have no complaints!

Next, make sure you schedule regular money "dates," whether they are quarterly, semi-annually, or annually...whatever works best for you and your hubby. Financial issues change over time, and you need to adjust your budget accordingly. Write down ahead of time what you want to discuss at your money dates. This may help avoid, or at least mitigate, heated arguments with your frugal hubby. If you can, have these "dates" off-site in a nice setting — a favorite restaurant or a weekend getaway. It's harder to disagree when there's good food, good wine, and beautiful surroundings!

Reduce the Price

This strategy is not for every wife, but believe us: it's practiced by many wives who are married to a frugal hubby. We're not recommending going overboard with your spending here, but if you know you've exceeded your hubby's price-point tolerance on a personal purchase and a small reduction in price will prevent needless arguments, what's the harm?

One wife told us she consistently reduces the price on items when she knows it's more than her hubby thinks she should spend. Even though he knows they can afford the additional dollars, which is a must if you use this strategy, his frugal nature will get him upset if she discloses the full price. She's pretty sure he's figured out that she does this, but he's happy to go along to maintain marital harmony.

Pay the Bills

Being in charge of the checking account is highly recommended if you're married to a frugal hubby. Remember, what he doesn't know won't hurt him! And why should you unnecessarily increase his blood pressure over silly things?

Don't worry. You don't have to be a financial genius to take over this responsibility, and now, with online banking, this task is even easier; you don't even have to balance the checkbook — it's done for you automatically! Your hubby will probably appreciate you taking over the financial reigns. It's one less task for him to do!

Separate Checking Accounts

If your hubby won't give up the financial reigns, having your own checking account is almost as good. If you both work, determine together who will be responsible for which household expenses and how the "leftovers" will be handled. If you don't work outside the home, make sure you are fairly "compensated" for your household contributions. These funds should be under your total control.

Do Something for Yourself!

If your household finances allow it, you each should have a "slush" fund that you can access with no questions asked by either spouse.

If he wants to be frugal with his fund, so be it, but if you want to spend money on "full-price" gifts for yourself or others, that's your prerogative!

Frugal Checklist

- ☑ *Look for Bargains*
- ☑ *Financial Planning 101*
- ☑ *Reduce the Price*
- ☑ *Pay the Bills*
- ☑ *Separate Checking Accounts*

Unromantic Hubby

"Marriage is a book of which the first chapter is written in poetry and the remaining chapters in prose."

—Beverley Nichols

I recently was cleaning out my closet when I came across a scrapbook I made during college. Page after page, I had kept little hand-drawn love letters that my future hubby had passed to me while we were studying together in the library. They reminded me how these small gestures filled me with love and excitement.

Here are some strategies to follow to keep the romance alive and to keep your hearts pounding for each other's company!

Unromantic Warning Signs

Will I Be Married to an Unromantic Hubby?

- Does he plan for special occasions or are you always in charge of the planning?
- Does he send you nice cards/notes?
- What about your birthday? Does he do something thoughtful?
- Are his gifts practical or sentimental?
- If you're already married, how did he propose?

Unromantic Strategies

Date Night

While you are officially Mr. and Mrs., you can recall those romantic times when you were dating by planning "date nights." On these date nights, talk about the things you did together that made you feel special when you were boyfriend and girlfriend and look at pictures of when you were dating. Vow to keep the excitement alive!

Mystery Night

The need to restore romance after you have been married for several years is just a fact of married life. Rather than wishing your spouse would take more initiative, try scheduling monthly "mystery nights."

Be sure to alternate responsibility for planning the evening on these "mystery nights." Don't criticize his plans, or he will definitely stop doing it entirely. Use the time to talk about your goals as a couple and take stock of how you complement each other. Truly listen to each other and summarize what you hear the other person saying.

Each of you needs positive strokes that often go by the wayside. Mystery night sets the stage for needed hugs and kisses!

Romantic Getaway

If possible, try to select a weekend getaway every three or four months. If you have kids, it is worth all the lists you will need to leave with the person who is caring for them while you are away. It's easy to find weekend getaways close to home by surfing the Internet or travel magazines online. Some local magazines in your area may feature entire issues devoted to romantic getaways. If you can't afford an entire weekend, you will be amazed at what even one evening can do to satisfy your romantic appetite!

Time without Kids

As much as you love your kids and find it difficult entrusting them to the care of others, make sure you spend time alone with your hubby. Hubbies quickly take a backseat to kids, because your kids' needs must be met to maintain routines. Often times, hubbies remain in the backseat and relinquish their rights so as not to rock the boat.

To get your hubby back in the driver's seat, schedule time away from the kids. Whether this time is a massage that you schedule together, a date night, or a weekend getaway, let your hubby know how important he is to you. Break a babysitter in early so both of you can look forward to alone time, when you can embrace each other and restore the romance!

Romantic Movies

We all need ways to escape our routines. One easy way is to watch romantic movies together. Don't just watch them together, though. Talk to each other about what you liked about the characters.

This is a safe way to discuss relationships without pointing the finger at your spouse. Don't use the time to criticize your spouse, or he will never watch a chick flick with you again!

Romantic Setting—Lights/Music/Fragrance

Men can be easily seduced, and they appreciate you taking the initiative to set the stage for romantic interludes. Create the ambiance for romantic interludes with candles, music, and a spritz of your perfume. Start this before kids arrive on the scene so you will both know how to get back into the romantic mood.

Love Notes

Surprise your hubby with scented notes containing short messages that show him how much you love him. Be specific rather than just saying, "I love you." Putting these notes either in his coat pocket or on a night table will keep the romance alive and might even prompt your hubby to write notes back to you!

Show Appreciation

Most hubbies see their role as that of providing for you and your family even if you are bringing in a salary as well. Taking your spouse for granted is a common theme in most marriages. One can't feel romantic if overwhelmed by the pressures inherent in maintaining stability in the household.

Give your spouse positive feedback and let him know how much you appreciate all the things he does for you and the family. Try to put yourself in his shoes and you will have an easier time showing your appreciation. Small gestures go a long way!

Do Something for Yourself!

You will soon learn, as all the wives from this survey reported, that men are not mind readers, as much as we would like them to be.

If you love getting flowers or candy, send him the web site for enrolling in the appropriate club where he gets a reminder each month to select a "gift" to send to you.

Unromantic Checklist

- ☑ *Date Night*
- ☑ *Mystery Night*
- ☑ *Romantic Getaway*
- ☑ *Time Without Kids*
- ☑ *Romantic Movies*
- ☑ *Romantic Setting*
- ☑ *Love Notes*
- ☑ *Show Appreciation*

Workaholic Hubby

"Many marriages are simply working partnerships between businessmen and housekeepers."
—Mignon McLaughlin

I grew up in a household where my father would open the back door precisely at 5:30 pm, greet my mom with a kiss, change his clothes, and then we would all sit down for dinner. From Monday through Friday, you could set your clocks on my father's arrival!

My married life took a different turn. Five-thirty would come and go. We started agreeing that 6:30 would be the time he would come home for dinner. Last-minute calls at 6:20 told me he would be late, then no calls at all, because he didn't want to hear my yelling or screaming.

With just the two of us, I didn't mind that much — it gave me a chance to unwind after work. But then came the kids. With the first one, I would bundle her up and we would meet my husband somewhere for dinner. We tried to do this once or twice a week.

But then the twins came. I found out that my nanny was stealing from us, and I decided to stop having help — wrong move. Meanwhile, my husband was working longer and longer hours. We tried negotiating for him to come home just two of the five days for dinner. That worked for a week and then disintegrated. He didn't want to come home to be bombarded by the yelling, and he had no idea, nor did he want to know, about the day I had with the kids. Finally it came down to Wednesday, figuring it would be smack in the middle of the week. To this day, with all the kids out of the house, my husband tries to reserve Wednesdays for dinner at home.

The moral of the story is this: Find your own ways to reschedule your workaholic hubby.

Workaholic Warning Signs

Will I Be Married to a Workaholic Hubby?

- What are his work habits like now?
- Is he married to his job?
- Does work seem to be his only interest, or does he have hobbies and other ways he likes to spend his time?
- Is he always bringing work home?
- Does he spend the majority of his time off working?
- When he's not working, does he worry that he should be working?
- Are you constantly rescheduling dates due to his work schedule?

Workaholic Strategies

Put Yourself on His Official Calendar

When married to a workaholic hubby, you need to find a way to bump yourself up on his list of priorities. One sure way is to make friends with his administrative assistant.

One wife and admin act as a team without her hubby even knowing it. Each week his admin e-mails his calendar to her with times and appointments so that the wife knows not only when her hubby is busy, but when there might be time for lunch, dinner, or just time to connect. In turn, the wife e-mails the admin important dates and times when her hubby needs to be available.

Book a Weekly Date

If your hubby doesn't have someone keeping his schedule, then you will need to find another way to get yourself on his calendar. Whatever you do, don't give up. Schedule some quiet time with your hubby to work out a few lunch or dinner "dates," or even phone calls, where he promises you will have his undivided attention.

If you start this early in your marriage, it will become a habit and not a chore for him. After 25 years of marriage, several wives have told us their heart rates still go up anticipating their rendezvous with their hubbies! Their hubbies concur!

Enlist the Kids

Early on in a marriage, both of you may tolerate the long hours that you spend apart hoping that you are advancing your careers. But "connect time" on a regular basis is critical to maintaining a happy, fulfilling marriage. It is also time that, if neglected, leads to disintegration of a marriage.

If you negotiate for certain times together in the beginning of the marriage and both commit to these times, you will find yourselves in a much better place when kids come on the scene. This way, you can avoid the resentment caused by just one of you holding down the fort, which often increases exponentially with each child.

One wife made certain that once a week she bundled her kids up and either took dinner to share with her hubby, or they went to a local restaurant. When the kids got older, she put them on the phone to plead with their dad to come home for dinner. Another wife had her kids draw up contracts with her hubby with things like, "If you're home by 6:30 pm, you'll receive coupons for hugs and kisses and drawings."

Negotiate Help

Resenting your hubby's long hours leads to thoughts of revenge and bitterness, which only makes the marriage suffer. Wives have reported that when their hubbies finally do come home, these wives are so angry that many times they either yell at their hubbies or they don't speak to them at all. Tired hubbies are not good at sympathizing with their wives, and this often leads to them coming home even later. After all, hubbies are getting strokes at the office for putting in their time.

Wives need to take charge to break this cycle. One successful strategy is finding people to lessen the load: bartering with relatives or friends or hiring help. Make a list of the activities that cause the most fatigue and figure out who might be able to help you. You should not feel guilty about taking this step. You need to remember that in order to be able to give, you need to "fill your own well."

Develop a Hobby

This strategy goes for both you and your hubby. You need to help your workaholic hubby find out that there is more to life than work. In fact, this strategy is one that is recommended on the Workaholics Anonymous Web site (www.workaholics-anonymous.org). Cultivating a hobby early in the marriage will allow your hubby to see that he can get pleasure from many different activities.

For many workaholics, their fear of failure drives them to work long hours. A hobby will not only allow your hubby to unwind, but also to experience the joy of accomplishing something non-work related. Developing a hobby is also a good idea for you, whether it is something you do on your own or with a group. Finding your own outlet that brings you joy will show you that you can derive happiness from things and people other than your hubby.

Time-Savers

Workaholic hubbies need help in adopting strategies that can save them time. Buy him a book on time management or read the book yourself and offer him some constructive ideas. Once again, he needs to see that he can succeed while being more efficient with his time.

Press the Delete

A workaholic hubby always thinks he can complete ten things, when in reality he only has time for five!

You won't be able to have him cut down his workload that drastically, but see if you can get him to "press the delete button" on at least one item on his list. A funny or romantic e-mail asking him to "press the delete" will put him in a good mood, as one wife reported.

Taking one item off his list will give him more time to spend with you, or at least to give you a call. If you remind him to do this at least three times a week, he will see the pleasure he gets and the pleasure you get from this small gesture.

Prioritize

If you are successful in having your hubby "press the delete button," you can point out to him that it is helpful to prioritize his to-do list and make one of his priorities his family. He need not set aside big blocks of time. Most wives report that they just want their hubbies to be fully engaged with them and not multi-tasking when they are together.

Wives who have explained to their hubbies upfront how much it means to them to have this time together, and how it hurts them when their hubbies are late or cancel at the last minute, have reported benefits from taking this simple action.

Do Something for Yourself!

You will be able to bring more happiness to your marriage if you engage in activities that you find pleasurable. Your feelings of self-worth and being needed by others will minimize your feelings of loneliness or self-doubts.

It is a tough pill to swallow, but you can't realize all your happiness from one individual, let alone your hubby.

Wives who have found their own outlets report that not only can they be more compassionate and empathetic toward their hubbies' schedules, but that they are more effective in communicating their concerns with their hubbies, as well.

Workaholic Checklist

- ☑ *Put Yourself on His Official Calendar*
- ☑ *Book a Weekly Date*
- ☑ *Enlist the Kids*
- ☑ *Negotiate Help*
- ☑ *Develop a Hobby*
- ☑ *Time-Savers*
- ☑ *Press the Delete*
- ☑ *Prioritize*

Time-Insensitive Hubby

"The task is to learn how to enjoy everyday life without diminishing other people's chances to enjoy theirs."

—Mihaly Csikszentmihalyi

I'm a planner by nature, so whenever I have to do a chore or be somewhere, I know exactly what I have to do to accomplish the task or get somewhere on time. I guess that's part of my upbringing. If my mother was entertaining, she started preparing (and freezing) weeks in advance so nothing had to be done last-minute. And whenever we had to be somewhere, my father calculated what time we had to leave to the exact minute so we would get there at least one-half hour early, sometimes even earlier.

Not so with my in-laws — what a clash of cultures! Nothing was planned, everything was last-minute and chaotic, and no one ever got anywhere on time. It got to the point that whenever the two families got together, my mother would tell them we were meeting at least 30 minutes earlier, and even then, they were still usually late!

You can reset your time-insensitive hubby's internal clock by following our time-tested strategies.

Time-Insensitive Warning Signs

Will I Be Married to a Time-Insensitive Hubby?

- Was he late for your first date? Other dates?
- Is he late for classes? Work?
- Does he miss appointments? Does he have to reschedule?
- Does he oversleep?
- Do his friends tell you they're always waiting for him?
- Are you constantly reminding him it's time to get going?

Time-Insensitive Strategies

Change the Time

Little white lies are okay if it helps get your hubby somewhere on time! You know that if left to his own devices, he won't arrive on time, so adjust the arrival time to mirror your hubby's bad habits. If he's usually a half hour late, then your appointment just became a half hour earlier! He'll catch on eventually, so make sure you use this tactic judiciously.

Change the Distance

You can achieve the same results as "Change the Time" by changing the distance. Tell your hubby that your appointments are further away than they actually are. Make sure you make the adjustment in proportion to the actual distance, however. For example, you can safely add 30 miles to a 300+ mile trip, but only 5 to 10 miles to an appointment that is just 20 miles away.

Early Warning System

Keep reminding him, and reminding him, and reminding him, about important appointments. Remind him early in the morning, four hours before, and one hour before the appointment. Do this as many times as it takes to get him there on time. Be careful, though — we've already heard "Why Nagging Doesn't Work." These reminders need to be gentle, well-timed, and well-spaced to be effective.

Arm the Alarm

You need to become techno-wife to carry out this strategy. Figure out how to set the alarm on his smart phone, or whatever he uses for a calendar/reminder system. Go ahead and program in all your important dates. Don't forget our first strategy, "Change the Time," when doing so!

Enlist His Staff

If your hubby has support staff, they're probably well aware of his time problems. While not all time-insensitive hubbies are also time insensitive at work, usually the same behaviors shown at home also exhibit themselves at the work place.

See if you can get someone on his staff on your side, especially when there's a really important weekday function. Ask this person for help getting him out of the office on time. This staff member could issue reminders a la "early warning signs" and make sure his calendar is clear close to send-off time. Be sure to let this person know how much you appreciate his help.

Change the Clocks

Every minute helps! Make sure all your house clocks and car clocks and his wristwatch are at least five minutes fast. One wife who successfully uses this strategy tells us that it's gotten so bad in their house that they never know what time it really is! Thank goodness for the clocks on cell phones and computers.

The 15-Minute Rule

While in college, the 15-minute rule means giving a professor 15 minutes' leeway before class is cancelled, at home it means to be 15 minutes early for everything.

Many hubbies just can't plan correctly to be somewhere on time. So if you subtract 15 minutes or more, depending how late he usually is, from your hubby's miscalculation, it should come out just about perfect!

If he arrives early, so much the better!

Trim the List

Most men are notorious planners and think they can do it all. Eliminating at least one activity he had planned to "squeeze" in before your big date could be all he needs to stay on track.

Do Something for Yourself!

Are you tired of having a reputation for being late all the time because of your delinquent hubby? You can control the timeliness of some of your arrivals and feel good about your efforts.

First, make sure you're on time — even early — for everything you do on your own. For joint engagements, if it's feasible, arrive separately and, of course, on time. You'll feel good that you're able to enjoy the entire party and won't be stressed out about planning for your hubby's arrival.

Time-Insensitive Checklist

- ☑ *Change the Time*
- ☑ *Change the Distance*
- ☑ *Early Warning System*
- ☑ *Arm the Alarm*
- ☑ *Enlist His Staff*
- ☑ *Change the Clocks*
- ☑ *The 15-Minute Rule*
- ☑ *Trim the List*

Messy Hubby

"Love is the thing that enables a woman to sing while she mops up the floor after her husband has walked across it in his barn boots."

—Hoosier Farmer

It's not that my husband doesn't want to be neat, or try to be neat. I don't think he can! First of all, he won't throw away anything. You never know when you might need it! I'm not just talking old college term papers, but the note cards he used to prepare the papers from.

If you look at my in-laws' basement, you could see the roots of my husband's problem. The items collected were incredible — old newspapers, magazines, books, clothes from the Dark Ages — items that no sane person would ever think of using. Sadly, my basement looks the same, and my garage, and my guest room, and my husband's closet.

And it's not like I'm a real neatnik, but it really does get to me when navigating through our hallways is like navigating through a land mine. What upsets me even more is he doesn't even notice the mess around him. His answer? We just have different tolerance levels. Very funny!

Will you be picking up after your messy hubby for the rest of your life? Not if you de-clutter your hubby using our strategies.

Messy Warning Signs

Will I Be Married to a Messy Hubby?

- Take a look around his current apartment/house. Is it well taken care of? Or is it a pigsty?
- Does he pick up after himself? Or expect you to do it?
- Does he put away his clothes, or are they strewn all over the house?
- What about the kitchen? Are there dirty dishes in the sink? Spoiled food in the refrigerator?
- What about his parents' home? Is it neat and orderly when you visit?
- If you knew him in college, how did he live then?
- Does he give anything away or is he a pack rat?

Messy Strategies

One Room at a Time

We know, we know...When living with a messy hubby, you just want the whole house clean now! Unfortunately, that's unrealistic. What may work is taking baby steps, either together or alone.

Target one room or area of the house at a time. Get that room under control, and then move on to the next. This approach may take a while, but you'll get a real sense of accomplishment with each new room you "conquer."

Negotiate

We're convinced that one of the reasons hubbies become messy is they can't throw anything, and we mean *anything*, away.

One wife told us that not only does her hubby have copies of all his old college papers, he also has copies of the note cards he used in writing the papers. Tell your messy hubby that enough is enough. He can't possibly keep (or use) everything he has, because there just isn't room. He has to choose. He can keep three out of every five items — that isn't bad!

Get Organized

Another reason hubbies become messy is their lack of organizational skills. What seems so easy for most wives, organizing, is just overwhelming for most messy hubbies. It's just not in their DNA; they're missing that "organizational gene."

Here's where you need to step in. If you can create a system for your messy hubby, some hubbies will gladly follow it. In fact, they may actually be relieved. Some messy hubbies don't want to be messy; they just don't know how not to be. Take the time to show them how to structure and label things. Something as simple as putting his dress socks in one drawer and sports socks in another may never occur to him.

One wife told us that every time she asks or begs her husband to clean up, he complies by building more storage "systems." The problem is that he doesn't sort through anything. He throws it all into closed, unmarked bins. Clearly this hubby needs help. Creating a system for your messy hubby will be time well spent.

Bag It, Hide It, Get Rid of It

If your hubby is messy because he can't part with his old clothes, this strategy might work for you.

One wife got this strategy from her mother-in-law. It seems that hanging on to old, out-of-date clothes was a long-time family tradition that was passed on from father to son. Her mother-in-law told her to take all the clothes her hubby didn't wear and hide them somewhere for six months. If he didn't miss them during that period, then it was safe to get rid of the clothes.

Use Laundry Baskets

"Why bother putting everything away when it will just get messed up anyway?" That's one wife's philosophy. She came up with the "laundry basket" strategy: Instead of putting her hubby's clothes in drawers, she lines up laundry baskets on the floor of their bedroom. One basket is for underwear and socks, one is for t-shirts, and another is for work-out clothes. You get the picture. Now she doesn't get upset about her hubby's drawers and closet being a mess, and her hubby likes this approach also — he just grabs his clothes and goes.

Call 1-800-Got-Junk?

If you're married to a messy hubby, you have plenty of junk. Here's a way to get rid of it, and fast. Whoever invented this concept was a genius! (Maybe they were married to a messy hubby.)

What's great about this approach is that it requires very little work on your part. You just pick up the phone and call. This organization, or others like it, will arrive with its own truck and workers to get rid of your junk, either by the hour or by the truckload. You just have to tell them what to take. What could be more fun than watching your junk disappear right before your eyes?

Now You're Doing Your Own Laundry

One of the most frustrating things about living with a messy hubby is all the extra laundry he creates. All his clothes become a wrinkled mess! If you're the chief "launderer" in your family and his clothes are messy here's a way to lay down the law:

Until he gets his mess under control, he needs to do his own laundry, from start to finish. This includes sorting, washing, folding, and putting it away. Who knows? After trying this for a few weeks, he might beg you to give him another chance. If this is the case, and you decide to give in to his pleas, make sure it's conditional: One messy pile of clothes, and he's back to doing his own laundry again!

Everything in the Middle of the Floor

If you're tired of picking up your hubby's belongings all over the house, try gathering them up and putting them in one large, visible pile. Leave his stuff there until he picks up everything himself.

Be aware that this strategy could backfire, however. One wife tried this and her husband just calmly stepped over the pile. Here's what he told her: The mess didn't bother him, because his standards were not as high as hers. Seriously? We think this is the exception, not the rule, however. Most messy hubbies will choose to remove their stuff from the middle of the room, especially if there are valuable items and kids or pets around.

The Man Cave

The "man cave" — one room in the house for all his belongings, that you don't have to clean, and don't even have to enter! Doesn't this sound heavenly? Let him have this "special" room for all his stuff, and you may be able to save the rest of your household.

Let us provide a word of caution, though, if you choose to go this route: This special room has to come with conditions. He has to take care of it himself; even though it can be messy, it has to be kept pest-free, which means that no food or other garbage can be left around. And the rest of the house is off-limits for any of his things.

Have a Garage Sale

America's favorite "cleaner upper" could help you get a messy hubby under control. The key to getting Messy involved, and willing to part with some of his cherished belongings, is to agree ahead of time to buy something he really wants with the proceeds of the sale. Watch how quickly his stuff hits the pavement or the garage.

Donate to Charity

A close cousin to the garage sale, donating to charity, can also help clear your household of unwanted items. First, find out what items are on some local charities' wish lists. Do they match some items in your messy hubby's collection? If so, show him that donating these items to charity will not only help a good cause, but will benefit him, as well — you'll show your gratitude when these items are finally out of the house! Many organizations will pick up the donations themselves and will also provide a receipt so that you can claim your donation as a tax deduction.

Do Something for Yourself!

When married to a messy hubby, walking into the house can be overwhelming if every room is a mess.

Make sure there are areas that are under your total control, and make those rooms your own personal haven.

Keep these rooms spotless. Keep your messy hubby out, or at least forbidden to mess anything up.

Sort of a reverse Man Cave; declare parts of the house off-limits to your messy hubby, and you'll enjoy every minute spent in your clutter-free oasis.

Messy Checklist

☑ *One Room at a Time*

☑ *Negotiate*

☑ *Get Organized*

☑ *Bag It, Hide It, Get Rid of It*

☑ *Use Laundry Baskets*

☑ *Call 1-800-Got-Junk?*

☑ *Now You're Doing Your Own Laundry*

☑ *Everything in the Middle of the Floor*

☑ *The Man Cave*

☑ *Have a Garage Sale*

☑ *Donate to Charity*

Cupid's Cheat Sheet (aka Rocks of Reality)

We thought the best way to end this book was to give you advice directly from the experts: our survey respondents, in their own words. We have grouped them under ten general categories that can apply to any and all hubby types! You can use Cupid's Cheat Sheet in a number of ways.

For newlyweds and soon-to-be-weds, this advice will help prepare you for entering marriage — not through rose-colored glasses, but with 20/20 vision, resulting from our experts' hindsight. We guarantee your honeymoon period will be extended!

For those married between five and ten years, this advice will help you right your course if you have temporarily lost your way and bring harmony back to your relationship.

For those married ten or more years, congratulations! You must be doing many things right in spite of the bumps and bruises you've endured. Reflecting on these "rocks of reality" will let you know you are not alone in your desire to pursue happiness. You may just pick up some insights that make you feel good about continuing your journey with your mate. That's just what we found!

Be Kind

"Husbands are like fires – they go out when they're left unattended."

—Cher

- *"I like the 'dog analogy.' Every time a dog sees you, he/she greets you with unconditional love and as if he/she hadn't seen you for days. Nothing makes a human being feel more loved than being greeted with enthusiasm and joy. It's a simple thing we can do for each other every day!"*
- *"Don't track who does what for each other; you have to want more for the other person than what you want for yourself."*
- *"Be more concerned about your spouse's happiness than your own."*
- *"Consider your hubby's feelings, even if you think he is being irrational."*
- *"Be your spouse's best friend."*

Be Flexible

"More marriages might survive if partners realized that sometimes the better comes after the worse."

—Doug Larson

* *"You must give and take; however, there must be one of you that is willing to give more."*
* *"Talk with options in mind."*
* *"Be willing to accept those things that may not change. Be willing to compromise and think of marriage as a partnership, with both people contributing to build a life together."*
* *"Sometimes it is better to give in on some issues than to be right all the way to divorce court."*
* *"We have been through some tough times, and neither one of us is the same person as when we married. The important thing is that we were flexible to roll with the punches."*

Be Independent

"A long marriage is two people trying to dance a duet and two solos at the same time."

—Anne Taylor Fleming

- *"Don't underestimate your own abilities."*
- *"Nurture your own activities and interests separate from your husband, and encourage him to do the same."*
- *"Girls, set aside some money that is your own to save for a rainy day (not just to spend)."*
- *"Be confident that you can make decisions without relying on his advice."*
- *"Make sure you always take care of yourself. Be self-confident and have self-respect."*

Respect and Support Each Other

"No, I don't understand my husband's theory of relativity, but I know my husband, and I know he can be trusted."

—Elsa Einstein

- *"Before getting upset, try and put yourself in your husband's place and see how you would like it if the table was turned around."*
- *"Disagree with respect."*
- *"Be there when you need each other."*
- *"A good marriage will always require work and the interest of both parties to keep it alive, fun, and romantic."*
- *"Build your marriage on a strong foundation of trust and love."*

Listen To Each Other

"I used to tell my husband that, if he could make me 'understand' something, it would be clear to all the other people in the country."

—Eleanor Roosevelt

- *"Listen to each other. Really listen and learn, and only give advice to each other if you ask it from one another. You can't listen and talk at the same time."*
- *"Acknowledge ALL areas of concern or things that bother you (or him) and be sure to address them early on."*
- *"Communicate and don't criticize."*
- *"Set aside some time to reassess your relationship every three months or four times a year."*
- *"Respect your spouse's point of view, even if you disagree with what is being said."*

Do Things Together

"Only choose in marriage a man whom you would choose as a friend if he were a woman."

—Joseph Joubert

- *"Do activities together and make sure that you have leisure-time activities in common. (Not just going out to eat.)"*
- *"Stay each other's best friend."*
- *"Share and enjoy common interests."*
- *"Always make time for each other."*
- *"Find things that you enjoy doing together and have 'special times' as a couple…Don't always be with friends when out together."*

Appreciate What You Have

"All that a husband or wife really wants is to be pitied a little, praised a little, and appreciated a little."

—Oliver Goldsmith

- *"Appreciate everything that you do have. Things may look perfect in someone else's world, but it never is; don't believe everything people tell you."*
- *"When you have trying times together, try to think about the good times, when you first fell in love."*
- *"Marry someone who will stand by you through thick and thin...If that doesn't work, keep your fingers crossed!"*
- *"The longer you are married, the more important it becomes not to take your spouse or relationship for granted."*
- *"View marriage as a challenge every single day, but one that is worth the work and aggravation."*

Keep Everything in Perspective

"Strike an average between what a woman thinks of her husband a month before she marries him and what she thinks of him a year afterward, and you will have the truth about him."

—H.L. Mencken

- *"Don't sweat the small stuff!"*
- *"Don't get married thinking you can change him; it doesn't work." Authors' note: This writer didn't have the benefit of reading this book!*
- *"View marriage as a work in progress."*
- *"Don't measure reality against the ideal... That almost always leads to unhappiness."*
- *"Try to look at the big picture... What is really important? The little stuff is just that... Little."*

Forgive and Forget

"Once a woman has forgiven her man, she must not reheat his sins for breakfast."

—Marlene Dietrich

- *"Don't be afraid to say 'I love you' or 'I am sorry.'"*
- *"Apologize and mean it."*
- *"Don't hold a grudge."*
- *"Try not to go to bed angry — it only ruins your sleep!"*
- *"Learn to forgive if someone makes a mistake."*

Talk, Talk, Talk

"A happy marriage is a long conversation which always seems too short."

—Andre Maurois

* *"Don't ever think that if he loves you enough, he will instinctively know what you want or need. It just doesn't happen! You have to TALK!"*
* *"Talk about what is working and what is not. Communicate honestly and openly."*
* *"Talk, don't criticize, and be patient."*
* *"Laugh with each other."*
* *"Address areas that bother you or him early on."*

Rocks of Reality Checklist

☑ *Be Kind*

☑ *Be Flexible*

☑ *Be Independent*

☑ *Respect and Support Each Other*

☑ *Listen to Each Other*

☑ *Do Things Together*

☑ *Appreciate What You Have*

☑ *Keep Everything in Perspective*

☑ *Forgive and Forget*

☑ *Talk! Talk! Talk!*

A Note from the Authors (Our Hubby Final Five)

You've read all our strategies. What more could we have to say? We wanted to leave you with one of our favorite anecdotes from our survey. Even after 30+ years of marriage, we refer to this one when we feel the pressure rising.

> *"One of my hubby's cousins said to me that she could easily think about all of the negative attributes of her hubby, but she CHOSE to instead focus on all his positive qualities."*

One last thing: We hope you'll find this book fun to read as well as practical, and we hope you'll find success with many of the strategies in this book. No matter what hubby type you've married, try to remember ***Our Hubby Final Five***: five overarching principles for living happily together.

❶ Talk with each other

Make time to talk with each other on a regular basis. Use some of your "couple's alone time" to check on each other's state of happiness in the marriage. Start out by telling your hubby the positives, and then mention what is bothering you. We don't mean to imply that you need to gripe every time you have some alone time, though. This would defeat the purpose and scare your hubby away from sharing time together.

❷ Nip "it" in the bud

Don't just think "it" will go away. Bad habits are difficult to break. Deal with small issues in a timely manner; don't let a mole hill become a mountain.

❸ Come up with solutions

Don't simply criticize his actions. Come up with solutions that both of you are willing to live with. You may need to compromise and also revisit the solutions to ensure their success.

❹ Listen to each other

Be open to the possibility that your hubby has legitimate reasons for his actions that he has not verbalized. Looking at issues from his perspective can help in both dealing with and resolving problem areas.

❺ Change your perspective

Remember, your marriage is not a sprint, but a marathon. You want to go the distance with your hubby. Remember your reasons for getting married, think of all of his good qualities, and appreciate the pressures you both might be under.

"Many marriages work better if the husband and wife clearly understood that they are on the same side."

—Zig Ziegler

Acknowledgements and Thanks

We are grateful to our wide network of family and friends, who assisted us with different elements of this book.

First, to the **married women** who completed the survey and shared their strategies for long-lasting marriages.

To our readers, **Angela Arnold, Joanna Walsh**, **Sean** and **Jessie Conta, Peggy Fox,** and **Marta Leipzig,** who helped tweak the contents and who bolstered our spirits that this book would be valuable to newlyweds, "olderweds," and soon-to-be-weds.

To **Stan Spector,** who shared his publishing expertise and gave us much-needed technical advice.

And finally, to our children**, Lacey** and **Jodie Gorochow**, who developed the concept for portraying our hubbies, to **Elana Rabinowitz** for her editing assistance, to **Jason Rabinowitz** for his marketing expertise, and to **Erica Gorochow** for creating the illustrations of our 10 challenging hubby types.

About the Authors

This book must work, as evidenced by the fact that the authors, our spouses, asked us to write their bios. Sure, we were honored, but it still takes an effort. Now, here is the proof that your purchase is a good investment: We didn't hesitate in getting this done. Why? After much experience, we know we are outmatched.

So, about our wives:

Beth met me when we were both in middle school. Although there was a five-year gap before we started dating again — not being able to drive put a real damper on the relationship — we reconnected in college and have been together ever since. Beth has worked all her life, mostly in marketing and business development. She still found time to earn a Master's degree in Public Administration and to raise our two children (and me). She was the ultimate sports mom while our kids were growing up, and she morphed into the ultimate sports fan. During the fall and winter she is a Bills and Giants fanatic and then switches to basketball to root for her beloved 'Cuse and Knicks.

Monica received her PhD in Health Psychology and has conducted research and given workshops on a variety of health topics. Over 20 years ago, Monica adjusted her mission statement to include the raising of our three (now grown) children. (I was there, too.) During that time, she remained connected to her profession, but has now re-immersed herself through her founding of a non-profit organization (VITAL, Inc.) that deals with issues of the aging population of baby boomers. Monica likes to travel and exercise, and as importantly, makes certain I travel and exercise as well. She has several close friends with whom she shares common experiences. At the top of that list is her co-author, Beth. This book has been a labor of love for both of them.

Finally, although we hate to admit it, we do recognize too many of the profiles within ourselves. The appeal of the book is universal because although we don't admit it, we are ordinary, average guys with ordinary, average experiences who have ordinary, average responses, making us one of many fitting subjects. But, through all of the years of marriage, our wives have made us feel neither ordinary nor average.

—Ken and Mitch

CPSIA information can be obtained at www.ICGtesting.com
Printed in the USA
LVOW122153180613

339211LV00003B/15/P